HOW TO BE
A GREAT SWIM PARENT

Praise for *How to Be A Great Swim Parent*

"Just when you thought that Coach Warner has written as much as he could about the world of competitive swimming he has once again written another must-read book.

How To Be A Great Swim Parent is more than just a book for our sport parents, it actually works for parents of children in all sports. It is also a book for coaches and even excerpts that can be shared with your swimmers. Coach Warner takes a step by step approach with the information that is so critical to help educate new swim parents but will also be very informative for the veteran parents on your club. When this book is published I plan to purchase at least a dozen to have all new parents read when they join the team. This is a quick read, an easy read but most importantly a MUST-READ."

—COACH IRA KLEIN, Head Coach Sarasota Tsunami, Board Member, USA Swimming

"Wow!! Just finished it. Coach Warner knows what it's all about. What a gift to have this as a resource for any parent or coach in any sport!

Coach Warner's ability to intermix stories with effective sports parenting lessons makes his guide an absolute pleasure to read. The downside I see is it may be mistaken as 'required reading' which would attach a perception that it is a chore. Oh, but quite the contrary in reality. *How To Be a Great Swim Parent* is an absolute joy to read. I will be making it available to our parents and coaches in our program every season! Thank you, Coach!"

—MIKE KOLEBER, Nitro Swimming, former Board President/Board Member, American Swimming Coaches Association

"Fantastic! Loved how you wove in so many real-life examples as well as published research with your own personal views and perspective. I hope lots of parents read this! Well done!"

—JENNIFER LAMONT, CEO of American Swimming Coaches Association

"Chuck Warner's book about being a great swim parent is a must-read for any parent with a child involved in competitive swimming. Warner's vast experience as a coach and parent shines through in this insightful and practical guide while leaning into insightful and relevant quotes from some of the best athletes and performers in the world.

The book covers various topics, from understanding the sport of swimming to navigating the challenges and rewards of being a swim parent. Warner provides valuable advice on supporting your child's swimming journey, including tips on communication, goal-setting, and maintaining a healthy balance between swimming and other aspects of life.

What I appreciated most about this book is Warner's emphasis on being a positive and supportive parent. He encourages parents to focus on their child's progress and personal growth rather than on winning or achieving specific outcomes. This perspective is refreshing and empowering, reminding parents that their role is to provide love and encouragement, not pressure and criticism.

I highly recommend it to anyone seeking guidance and inspiration to be the best swim parent possible."

—MIKE MURRAY, President, American Swimming Coaches Association, Head Coach, The Victor Swim Club

"Whether you are a swimming parent or coach, this book will become your 'go-to' in navigating your athlete through youth sports participation.

With more than four decades of experience, Coach Warner speaks plainly about how to best support your swimmer. He teaches us to learn to appreciate progress, belief in the process, and the power of perseverance.

I highly recommend this read! As a longtime club Coach, I can say that this is the parent education piece that we all wish we'd had for years! I plan on sharing this to new swim families as a standard part of our team welcome."

—KATHLEEN PRINDLE, Head Coach/Founder, Performance Aquatics, Board Member, USA Swimming

"Whether you are new to the sport, like me, or your family has been swimming for generations, there is something in this book for everyone. Coach Warner adeptly provides a road map for navigating the ups and downs of each swimmer's grueling journey, as seen through the eyes of the parent. Easy to digest tenets, stories and personal reflections allow the reader to see themselves in the narrative and makes the dialog tangible and personal. Every parent wants to support their child, but the 'how' very rarely comes from a Hall of Fame coach and mentor in the sport. Applying the ideas and anecdotes in this book has helped swimming bring my daughter and I closer. I will keep this book in my 'parental swim bag' for as long as my daughter competes."

—RICHARD QUAD, First Generation Swim Parent

"Coach Warner has done it again!

This book is a must-read for any parent who aspires to support their child as a developing athlete. His practical wisdom is born from a lifetime of experience as a parent and coach. Chuck reminds us that we use sport as a vehicle to teach life skills that transcend sport. The lessons and stories shared remind us about 'what matters most' as we work to give our children opportunities to grow to their potential in and out of the pool. As a parent of four athletic children and a lifelong swim coach, I can't imagine a better resource to help us focus on the 'right things' as we support the development of a young mind and body."

—MICKEY WENDER, Head Coach, Colorado Mesa University, 2024 NCAA DII Coach of the Year

HOW TO BE A GREAT SWIM PARENT

CHUCK WARNER

LUMINARE PRESS
WWW.LUMINAREPRESS.COM

How To Be a Great Swim Parent
Copyright © 2024 by Chuck Warner

All rights reserved. This book or any portion thereof may not be reproduced or used in any manner whatsoever without the express written permission of the publisher, except for the use of brief quotations in a book review.

Printed in the United States of America

Luminare Press
442 Charnelton St.
Eugene, OR 97401
www.luminarepress.com

LCCN: 2024913625
ISBN: 979-8-88679-636-0

Dedication

To every child entering the muffled calm of water and chooses to explore competitive swimming. And to your parents that love you so much, they picked up this book to seek information to help you gain the most from your experience.

To the life of the late Jon Urbanchek, who fifty years ago invited me to a seminar called "Action for Excellence" that changed my life, my daughter's life, and that of all the swimmers I've coached by introducing me to the nuts and bolts of self-image psychology articulated in this book.

To the life of the late Brent Rutemiller. Few people have ever intended so much good for so many people in the sport of competitive swimming. Blessed are those of us who befriended you.

Contents

Foreword . . . . *xiii*
Preface . . . . *xv*

   CHAPTER 1
Why Competitive Swimming? 1

   CHAPTER 2
Support, Don't Lead 5

   CHAPTER 3
Characteristics of a Champion Swimmer 13

   CHAPTER 4
Social Media 33

   CHAPTER 5
Theory of Desirable Difficulty 37

   CHAPTER 6
Create Opportunities, Not Obligations 43

   CHAPTER 7
Coach Life, Not Swimming 45

   CHAPTER 8
Parenting Is a Contact Sport 49

   CHAPTER 9
Don't Sell Your Kid Short 53

   CHAPTER 10
Beware of Destination Disease 55

Epilogue	61
Acknowledgments	63
Questions and Answers	67
About the Author	71
Other Books by Chuck Warner	73

Foreword

Congratulations on supporting your child to swim competitively! I coached college swimming for thirty-two years and can honestly say there is not a better group of friends for your child to have than the people they will meet through swimming.

What Chuck Warner provides you in these pages is a guidebook full of common wisdom, sprinkled with some science, plus his own coaching experiences spanning decades of success at every level of swimming.

This book is not about what *not to do* as a swim parent. From the first page Chuck invites you to partner with coaches and your swimmer to help your child find success and fulfillment on their journey. This is also not a book about how to help your child become an Olympic swimmer. It's better than that. It's a guidebook that can result in high-level family relationships as your swimmer navigates the challenges and triumphs of competitive swimming.

Also, if you didn't know, Chuck is one of the foremost chroniclers of American swimming history, having published books spanning the decades from the 1976 Olympics (*Four Champions, One Gold Medal*) through *...And Then They Won Gold: Stepping Stones to Swimming Excellence*, to the unparalleled career of coach Eddie Reese at the University of Texas, who retired in 2024, in *EDDIE REESE: Coaching Swimming, Teaching Life*.

So let Chuck Warner be your coach. And enjoy the ride.

Casey Converse
1976 USA Olympic Swim Team
Head Swim Coach, United States Air Force Academy 1988-2017

Preface

Each of us has been influenced by our parents on how to and how *not* to raise our children. As adults we have further molded our parenting philosophies based on our life experiences. What follows is a collection of observations and advice. I've accumulated this wisdom from a combination of being a child on swim teams, coach of swimmers and parents for fifty years, conductor of camps and clinics, researcher and author of three previous books, and most importantly, being a father and all that has taught me.

For twenty-four years I conducted a summer swim camp. Most of those years were while I was coaching both men and women at Rutgers University. On the first evening of each camp, we separated the parents from their children, and I provided a presentation to them entitled: "*How to Be a Great Swim Parent.*" One year, a parent stood up, stopped me, and turned to the one-hundred-plus parents in the room. He said, "This is my seventh year listening to Coach Warner's talk. I had one child at his camp for four years, now my second child is in her third year. Every year that I listen to this talk, I become a much better parent for at least three months (laughter). Then I start slipping (more laughter). I encourage you to listen and learn."

I loved speaking with camp parents whose children I was not coaching on a day-to-day basis like I did when coaching clubs. The reason is that whenever I spoke with the parents of my club swimmers, I felt that some of those moms and dads were suspicious of what I was trying to get them to do: drive their kids to practice more often, help run swim meets, raise money, etc. I think the camp parents, whom I might never see again, understood that my motives were purely for the benefit of their child and of them as parents. They understood that I was simply trying to provide a service so they could help their children have a better experience swimming.

Thus, my intention to serve the parent, as well as the child, is why I've written this book. My goal is that these thoughts will allow you to enjoy a better experience with your child within and outside the sport of swimming. There is significant detail in this book that you may wish to skim or even skip (in particular in chapter three, but please do read the section on self-image) and still gain a great deal by focusing more on the areas you're most interested in.

CHAPTER 1

Why Competitive Swimming?

"Know yourself and you will win all battles."
—Lao Tzu

The reasons to have your child in competitive swimming are voluminous. This short list captures some of the bigger concepts that may well convince you of the value of the wonderful decision you've made to support your child or children in the pursuit of swimming as fast as they are able.

The cleanest kids in town! Chlorine may not kill every surface infection, but it sure slows them from spreading. From washing the dirt off their feet and from under their toenails or discouraging the spread of many diseases (including COVID-19), you're going to have a sparkling clean kid!

Extraordinary cardiovascular development. Regardless of how fast your swimmer ultimately becomes, if they go to practice and apply themselves their capillary beds will be popping like fireworks on the Fourth of July! The long-term benefits of exercising, including strong cardiovascular systems, will be a powerful deterrent to heart and lung disease throughout their life.

Equal gender opportunities. The same choices of events by distance and stroke are offered for girls and for boys, from starting out, through the Olympics. Further, as a coed sport, the training of girls and boys together teaches respect for one another as training partners and teammates.

Like-minded friends. From carpool and locker room interaction, chats between races, and cheering for teammates, your daughter or son will make lifelong relationships with other children who are also active, energetic peers. As a parent, you can benefit from forming new friendships with other parents who value the benefits to their children that are inherent in the sport of swimming.

Improved personal best times. Each swimmer records a time for each of their events and distances. Each record becomes a personal standard (or PB, for *personal best*) that measures their improvement against their best performance. Almost no other sport can offer this objective standard of progression.

Delayed Gratification. In the 1970s, Stanford University Professor Walter Mischel led a study of delayed gratification, now commonly known as the *marshmallow experiment.* A choice was offered to children age four or five between eating one marshmallow at the moment or two after a fifteen-minute wait. When the professor followed up with a study years later with the same children, he found that those who had been willing to wait fifteen minutes for the two marshmallows tended to have better life skills (as measured by SAT scores, educational success, body mass index, and other positive life outcomes).

Improvement in the sport of swimming demands an investment of work and some amount of elapsed time before the results of that work will be evident. Children who are patient enough to train diligently in the present, for results that are not quickly seen, will gain lifelong benefits.

As your child reaches adolescence, weekly and monthly training goals will become more appealing, just as they do to most successful swimmers. If your child doesn't have elite swimming talent, and those training goals aren't enough to keep them motivated during a ten- to twenty-week season, they might be better off in a team sport where baskets, goals, or touchdowns are scored every few minutes. In swimming, when either a parent or a child looks for short-term (weekly or monthly) race improvements, the outcome is generally disappointed parents and a sad child. Equally important, those unrealistic expectations will decrease the likelihood of a child learning the value of delayed gratification from sustained, challenging work.

Use your powers or lose your powers. In the late 1970s a series of studies were conducted by psychologists at Simon Fraser University in British Columbia, Canada. The researchers created two environments for rats. One setting could be called Rat Prison. Resident rats had a basic cage with no frills. There was access only to a chemical stimulant, food, and water.

A second environment was created that could be called Rat Park. It contained a wheel to run on and places to explore, essentially offering the rats many activities they normally enjoyed. Rat Park offered the same options for food and water, and just like Rat Prison, a chemical stimulant. It wasn't long before the researchers found that the rats in Rat Prison were addicted to the chemical stimulant, while those in Rat Park were not interested in the chemicals at all.

The study concluded that because the inhabitants of Rat

Prison did not have the opportunity to use a broad scope of their natural abilities (their *powers*) to fulfill their lives, they became reliant on the chemical stimulant. Humans, like rats, will use their powers or lose their powers. We witness the same phenomena in the decay of a boat that sits idle, a car that is not started for days, neglected homes, human bodies that are not exercised, and minds that are not challenged. In all these examples, when there is no use of the capacity of the person or object, the result is decay.

For your child to reach their potential in the sport of swimming, they will need to use all their physical, mental, and spiritual abilities. Improvements in a swimmer's personal best times will come more rapidly when the athlete gives maximum effort both mentally and physically. Also, unique to the sport, your child will have a personal best time to improve upon in various distances and strokes and the individual medley. This combination of a swimmer's full engagement and its exploration through a variety of options for measured outcomes makes an easy argument that swimming is the best sport in the world for a child's development.

CHAPTER 2

Support, Don't Lead

"Support, don't lead your child into swimming."
—Coach Peter Daland, Olympic Swim Coach

Your child should be a swimmer because *they* want to be. A parent *leading* a child into swimming can only be effective if it is a short-term introduction. In the long run, your child will need to learn to swim for themselves to sustain a career in the sport that lasts through college or even through their high school years.

Yes, most young children will cooperate with their parents' initial leadership into a sport. But if you are the one supplying the motivation month after month, your child will not last long. By playing a supportive rather than leading role, you can coach them in the life skills they will need to get the most out of their swimming experience. This book is intended to show parents how they can most effectively *support* their child. It will also point out the pitfalls of trying to *lead* them through the experience.

The initial focus of support for your child is to be sure they know you believe in their coach. It takes a special mindset for your child to want to apply themselves in a sport that seven-time Olympic coach Eddie Reese describes this way:

Swimming is too hard for most people. You wake up earlier than you want. Work out longer than you want. Do it more frequently than you'd like. Don't have more than a few minutes to socialize during a workout. And you end your workout where you started! Just a lot more tired.

To commit to the work necessary to be successful, swimmers need to trust the leadership of their coach.

The leadership role the coach is hired to perform includes establishing expectations for practice (training) and competitions. The children who have the best experience in competitive swimming forge a partnership with their coach. The coach becomes the leader, and the swimmer becomes a willing follower, giving the coach feedback in the collaborative process of improving their swimming. A parent inserting themselves into this partnership by questioning their child's start or turn or other technique, is like an auto mechanic telling a dentist how to clean their child's teeth. Both professionals have unique skills, but they are not a match. While you are your child's trusted role model in life, your sports organization pays the coach to lead your swimmer and the team for a good reason.

Swim coaches are often professionals, unlike in most other youth sports. Be open-minded and learn about what your child's coach is planning for your swimmer. Many coaches will explain to parents their expectations for their children through annual meetings, newsletters, and other direct forms of communication. Be sure to attend, read, and listen. As your child talks about their experiences, you will learn more about the coach's expectations.

It's possible that your philosophy of how your child should be involved in youth sports will differ with the coaches' expectations for participation in practice, competitions, and possible parent-support activities. You will have to weigh what you can and cannot live with. If the conflicts are more than you are willing to accept, talk with the coach about it, especially when your child is age twelve and younger. This will strengthen your child's feeling that you support their leader, rather than putting them in the middle of a potential conflict. As you educate yourself about team policies and coach expectations, your teenage child should be able to take over most of the communication about questions you have for their coach.

When my daughter was approaching her teen years, the minister at our church told me that she was going to be looking for mentors other than her parents. He said the key was to make sure that she had good ones. That was sage advice.

Good coaches who provide positive leadership for your child can be life-changing mentors. But your support of the coach should never be given blindly, no matter how much your child reveres a new mentor. If what you hear from your child about your coach bothers you, then consider speaking privately with the coach. Consider what issue would be disturbing enough to take that step.

You have every right to expect your child to be safe and treated with dignity while in the care of a coach. If you don't believe your child's coach is providing that environment, and you're not satisfied with the results of that private conversation, then a next step could be to speak with the sports organization's board of directors or those in charge of hiring the coach.

If conversations with your child's coach or the club's leadership do not satisfy you, then you may have to consider moving your child to a different program. However, before you seriously consider that step, do a lot of homework. Parents that go *club hopping* are often doing their children a disservice. Be sure the new environment is going to have a clear net positive for your child.

If you are fortunate enough to have professional, positive, and well-educated coaches around your child, you are in for an extraordinary experience. Your support of the coach will make it easier for your swimmer. Their coach is trying to instill in your child the desire to attend practice regularly and apply themselves physically and mentally at each session. Sometimes, the work may be boring and occasionally it will be exhausting. Consequently, there will be days when your child gets in the car after practice tired and discouraged. Their mood in that moment may prompt them to complain.

It is wise to not give in to the temptation to join a blame game, especially if it pertains to their coach. Listen patiently. If they complain, think through your response. Your go-to question in these difficult moments could be "What did your coach say?" Simply asking this question demonstrates that you respect what their coach is thinking and planning. Listen to your child's answer. You may not understand all of what they are telling you, but your positive tone will support your child's confidence in their coach.

The most basic level of support for your swimmer—and perhaps the most fun experience—is to take your turn driving in a carpool. Working out an agreement, with another family or two that live nearby, to share in the driving to and from swim practice or swim meets has three clear benefits.

First, you will spend less of your own time and expense driving. Second, your child will have the chance to get to know teammates in a richer way than only by attending swim meets or through their greetings before and after practice. Third, if you just drive and listen, you will gain many insights into their swimming experience as well as school and other activities. If you can prohibit cell phones and earbuds, you will discover an amazing source of entertainment!

Even after a long day at work, I loved driving my daughter's carpool a few times a week. One night after practice, a ten-year-old carpool member and I were waiting in the hall for his brother and my daughter to finish dressing. Jack had his head down, looking at the floor, and was kicking his heels against the wall. I nudged him, looking for what was bothering him. He said, "I think if they would teach me something, I could be good at this."

Jack was having a negative experience because of his coaches. His feelings summarized that his practice group was just swimming up and down the pool, with little correction of technique or skills. His coaches did not show excitement for him and his teammates when they gave a good effort. Since I was a successful swim coach by profession, but busy coaching my own university team, being a regular volunteer coach did not seem to be a role I could assume. I surmised that the best course of action for me to take, in this case, was to accept the invitation of my daughter's coach to be guest coach for a night. Hopefully, I could teach the staff a more effective way to lead the team.

On the night of my guest spot, I was especially energetic. I marched up and down the pool deck calling names, making skill corrections, and enthusiastically recognizing individuals who were listening intently to me and applying themselves. During the carpool home it was unusually quiet. I wondered what my three passengers were thinking about my guest spot, but no one mentioned a word of it. We dropped the boys off. As soon as they got out, and the car door closed, my daughter turned from her passenger seat and without warning, introduction, or clarification of the subject she was addressing, blurted out, "That was *awesome!*"

Unfortunately, the example I tried to set did not draw out similar efforts from the staff, at least not as often as I would have hoped. One of the boys continued through a long, accomplished career in swimming, including competing for four years of college. My daughter devoted herself to competitive dance when she was thirteen and stopped swimming. Jack didn't last long before he devoted all his nonacademic time to baseball. Today, he is an executive for a major league baseball team. As for me, I will always remember them as a favorite carpool.

Might they have lasted longer in swimming if their coach had taught more and showed more enthusiasm in their training? Probably. But they would have surely stopped sooner if their parents had been trying to lead them through their experience as a swimmer instead of supporting them.

There are many necessary support tasks that help a swim team function effectively. Seldom does one individual do the critical work to support an organization. Rather, a *team* of parents does, each filling a vital role. The top end of one of those roles could be to serve on a board of directors or structured booster group. Every team needs officials, timers, and clerical staff for swim meets. Your contribution can be as simple as affixing the names of award winners on ribbons.

In addition to making the support group work, giving

your time shows your swimmer that you are committed to their experience. A bonus to volunteering your time is that you are likely to enjoy making some new friends.

If you like *thinking big* and have an interest in leading positive change for your family and your community, there is a place for you, too. At the YMCA in Wilton, Connecticut, Coach Dave Reilly started a fifty-meter pool committee to pursue building a much bigger facility than the old six-lane, twenty-five-yard pool the team was crowded into. Dave left a few years later, but I continued the fifty-meter pool committee for another four years. When I moved on, the new head coach, Tim Murphy, picked it up. A few years later, a new, outdoor, fifty-meter pool was constructed, with a bubble for the winter months.

If the series of head coaches had not sustained this effort, the pool would not have been built. Coaches could see the benefit to the community and team beyond their own tenure. In the same way, if the Wilton parents group limited their interest to their own children's high school years, the pool probably would not have been built either. By the time it was complete, their children were off to college.

There are two types of people needed to make big things happen—like building a new pool: generous people with deep financial resources, and people who can look beyond the needs of their children to serve the future of the community. The people in the Wilton area were fortunate to have a few key parents with both qualities.

Volunteering your time to not only support your child but also the team and community is an aspect of being an especially great swim parent. Few efforts can be more personally rewarding.

CHAPTER 3

Characteristics of a Champion Swimmer

"Solutions [success formulas] should be as simple as possible, but no simpler."
—ALBERT EINSTEIN

When I was a young coach, a prominent mentor told me that the three qualities to becoming a great swimmer were talent, opportunity, and hard work. As I gained experience as a coach and researched my first book, *Four Champions, One Gold Medal,* I found those three qualities too simple. Einstein was right when he suggested that "Solutions or success formulas…" are sometimes complicated. What follows is a discussion of the key characteristics of champion swimmers.

Before explaining the pyramid below, it's worth commenting that birth order can significantly affect your child's personality. For example, if you are the parent of multiple children, consider the stress you experienced caring for your first baby, compared to your second or third. With experience, you raised your comfort level for being the parent of a newborn. Your second or third child had a different entrance into the world than your first.

An article, "Law and (Birth) Order," published on March 2, 1985 in the *New York Times* provides this data: Since 1789, there have been 102 Supreme Court justices. By normal odds, one might expect one-third of the total (about thirty-four justices) would be the youngest, one-third the middle, and one-third the oldest child. Actually, fifty-six have either been the firstborn or an only child. Only nineteen were the baby of the family. An additional compelling fact is that twenty-one of NASA's first twenty-three astronauts were first-born children.

Studies related to birth order, such as those documented in Kevin McGuire's 2015 work for the University of North Carolina Law and Society Review, find that first-borns tend to be stronger in math, science, and law, while youngest children are often more successful in the creative areas of arts, sales, and comedy. One of the reasons attributed to this tendency is that firstborn children spend more time as the sole focus of their parents. Birth order can make a difference in your child's interests. It can also affect their personality (see below under *competitiveness*).

Birth order can influence a child's personality, but there are many other factors that influence it. As Yogi Berra said: "Every now and then, a reporter who thinks he is Freud asks me if being the youngest is why I made it. I almost always say, 'Yes, but I don't think it had anything to do with it.'"

The characteristics of a champion swimmer can be organized in the pyramid below. I have found that the three core building blocks of a successful competitive swimmer are at the base of the pyramid.

Competitiveness

When I was engaged in the research for *Four Champions, One Gold Medal,* I noted that each of the four champions was the youngest child in their family. Younger children tend to be organically engaged in competition with their older siblings. The competition starts subtly and almost immediately. Younger children hustle for bread on the dinner table, a preferred car seat, or their choice of a program on TV.

Consider the family makeup of two of the greatest swimmers in history. Michael Phelps has two older sisters who were world-class swimmers. Katie Ledecky is the youngest of two. This is not particular to swimming; for instance, basketball legend Michael Jordan has three older siblings. Many, many successful athletes started chasing their older brothers or sisters as a first engagement in competition.

Do you only have one child? Me, too. You can cultivate their competitiveness by creating competitive challenges. A feigned race around the house, between Mom or Dad, to get to the child's bedroom first to say good night, can help your child's introduction to competition. Especially if you grant them a victory when you see them give a maximum effort to win. When my daughter was five years old, I would stack the Chutes and Ladders deck of cards in her favor to encourage her appetite for winning. Two decades later, she continues to be a terror at board games, always expecting to win.

Pat King is a past president of the Orlando Magic, a National Basketball Association (NBA) franchise. King explains that there are *competitors* in the NBA who enjoy winning and will work to produce that outcome. He points out that there are also *predators*. Mr. King observed that these players loved competition so much, they will go to great lengths to seek out challenges, in most areas of their lives, to experience the adrenaline rush of competing. The result is often an ingrained habit of winning. King uses the examples of Michael Jordan and Larry Bird as predators that would feed their competitive juices by finding a *game within a game*. For example, they set goals for a scoring record in a building they played in or told players on an opposing team where they would shoot a game winning shot and then do it. These predators picked up on any comment by an opponent to fuel their fire.

Michael Phelps could be characterized as a predator. As an age-group (twelve and younger) swimmer, Michael first excelled at butterfly. When he was fifteen, he qualified to swim the two-hundred-meter butterfly at the 2000 Olympics in Sydney. Before his second Olympics in 2004, he focused his sights on Ian Thorpe, who most considered to be the best male swimmer in the world. The problem was, Ian's specialty was not butterfly, it was freestyle. So, Phelps worked to improve his freestyle so that he could race the Thorpedo in the two-hundred-meter freestyle at the 2004 Games. Although Michael came up short, eventually he set the world record in the two-hundred-meter freestyle in Beijing in 2008 adding that gold medal to the total of eight he would ultimately win.

The more competitive fire your child has, the more likely they are going to succeed in the sport of swimming. Should you happen to have a predator, hold on to your seat and enjoy the ride. Try to give them all the possible opportunities you can for good coaching and high-level competitive experiences.

Talent

There are many talent or physical assets that might contribute to your child's potential as a swimmer. Few people are at the top of the scale in every area.

- Height: Do you know the last time a world record was set in a freestyle event by a male under six feet tall? In 1977, five-foot-eight Brian Goodell set a world record in the four-hundred-meter freestyle. Why was it so long ago? The longer the vessel, the faster it tends to travel through the water, and the world's best swimmers are becoming taller and faster.

- Foot size: Just like fins on a swimmer, if your child has feet the size of Michael Phelps at size fourteen or Ian Thorpe at size seventeen, they give an advantage.

- Hand size: Just like bigger feet, bigger hands make bigger paddles and are an advantage.

- Arm length: Normally, a person's wingspan (arms outstretched, fingertips to fingertips) is about the same as their height. When a person's wingspan is wider than they are tall, it provides abnormally long *arm paddles.*

- White or red muscle fiber: White is explosive (rapid contractions, short duration), red has more blood and oxygen running through it (slower contractions, but greater endurance). Swimming has events for both types. There are short events for white-fiber dominant swimmers, but there are also endurance events that a red-fiber dominant athlete can excel in.

- Joint flexibility and stability: Looser joints can enable a swimmer to increase their *grip* or *hold* on the water. They enable swimmers' levers (hands, forearms and upper arms) to press the water at more advantageous angles and for a longer time. However, the ideal swimmer has both joint flexibility and joint stability. Stability is critical for avoiding injury and can be increased through rotator cuff strengthening exercises.

- Touch and feel for the water: This characteristic is noticeable when you are watching a race and say to yourself, "That person's swimming looks so *smooth* and *easy!*" The *feel for the water* gift tends to be genetic, so if your child does not have it, who is responsible? Frequent periods of sculling (sweeping motions with hands and forearms) can significantly improve one's feel for the water.

- Ankle flexibility: If feet turn out easily (eversion),

that is a breaststroke advantage. If they point straight back (or are pigeon toed), that is advantageous for freestyle, backstroke, and butterfly. The sport of swimming has something for everyone.

- Pain tolerance: Work works. This is especially true in preparing for endurance events. Pain is a "paper tiger" (see quote below) which can prevent or inhibit a fearful swimmer or less confident swimmer from progressing but can enable anyone willing to push through training pain to improve. How do you know if it is bad pain or injury pain? Generally, a bad pain is when the swimmer points at one specific spot to show where it hurts. When training, everyone will have a general feeling of pain, which is good.

"Each and every day you know that somewhere in that evening's main set, he (pain personified) will be waiting for you–looming. Go after him. Look him right in the eyes, and don't back down. Don't be fooled by the look on his face that he has 'your number'…it's a facade. He's a paper tiger. Blow right through him."
—Tim Shaw, 1975 Sullivan Award Winner

Opportunity

Many times, parents (and coaches) will view opportunity as a fifty-meter pool to train in. Fine facilities, however, are far down the list of priorities for your child to thrive in the sport.

The sport is delivered to your child by the coach. Even if the facilities are less than ideal (most are), your child can thrive if the coach is a good role model, who joyously and enthusiastically provides cutting-edge knowledge to their team. A good coach will have a developmental plan that will help your swimmer progress from one level to the next. It is the *coach* who is of greatest significance and is most critical to your child's opportunity to improve and progress.

Having time and space to practice is of importance as well. When your child is beginning at age seven to ten, a good coach will make optimum use of a few hours a week in the pool to teach technique and introduce conditioning. If your child is going to have a chance to be a national or world-class swimmer, at eleven to twelve years of age they will need much more training time. Seventy-five to ninety minutes of training six days a week, ten months a year, is likely the minimum to reach their potential in high school and college.

In addition, your child will benefit if there are teammates who challenge them in practice and competition. This does not mean that your child cannot be the best swimmer on the team of their age, because they can always be challenged in practice by older teammates. But it is important for them to swim in competitions where they will not win every race. Good, appropriate competition, along with parent support and support from the child's coach, will open a swimmer's eyes to how fast their peers are. If your son or daughter is competitive, racing against, and even losing to, swimmers their age can spur them on to improve their outcome the next time they encounter such an experience.

Self-image

Apple founder Steve Jobs was six years old and playing on his front lawn with his neighbor's daughter. The little girl said to Steve, "You're adopted! Those aren't really your parents." Steve raced into the house to confront his mother and father with this startling news. They said, "Yes, you are adopted, Steve. We picked *you*! You were that special to us, Steve. We picked *you*."

Very quickly, Steve's parents changed his perception of adoption from abandonment to being precious, loved, and wanted. The thoughtful words chosen by Steve's parents were something that helped propel him forward to be one of the most socially impactful people in history. Steve's parents helped their son take an early fork in the road toward a stronger self-image.

Self-image, sometimes called SI, is the picture we have of ourselves in our minds that affects our ability to perform a particular activity. For example, one might have a positive self-image in academics and a negative self-image in sports. Or one might see themselves as skilled in math but not in writing. For most of us, self-image is different for each unique activity in which we engage. In swimming, most children have a different self-image for freestyle than for breaststroke or for sprint versus distance races.

The human condition moves toward and becomes what we think about all day long. The picture of ourselves (our self-image) that dominates our thoughts and our self-esteem, leads us to our intentional or unintentional reality. This is why Mother Teresa attended peace or love rallies rather than anti-war rallies. She understood the power of thought and feelings and chose to direct her own toward a *positive outcome* rather than an outcome that avoids something negative.

If your thinking is stinking, your swimming performance will suffer. Put another way, winners see what they want, losers see what they are trying to avoid. Self-image is like the thermostat in a room: turn it higher, and the temperature moves upward. Lower your self-image, and your performance will follow downward.

There are two ways to improve self-image. One is to have positive experiences that lead to good feelings about performance in an activity. Consider, for example, how a student might feel when they write a paper in English class and receive a higher grade than what they expected. If this happens a few times, that student will likely start seeing themselves as better at writing papers than previously.

In competitive swimming, performance can raise a swimmer's self-image if they are so well-prepared that they cannot help but swim faster. For example, when I was fourteen years old, I was getting closer and closer to *breaking a minute* in the one-hundred-yard freestyle. This is a personal milestone for many swimmers. I can still remember—after several close calls of swimming the distance in 1:00 or 1:01—completing the last length of a race and thinking, "Not another 1:00, come on, not another one!" That was stinking thinking. I never swam a time of fifty-nine seconds. But one day, I did swim fifty-eight seconds for the distance. I just could not help but go faster because of my diligent training. Surely, one would expect to swim the distance in fifty-nine seconds long before swimming at a time of 0.58, but once my self-image locked onto 0.58, I never again swam a 1:00 in competition.

The second way to improve self-image is with words from experts that trigger pictures because pictures trigger emotions that elicit relevant feelings. Your child has people all around them that they consider to be experts; and thus, when the experts speak to your child, they contribute to your child's self-image. The two biggest experts in your swimmer's sport should be their coach and themselves. Hopefully, their coach understands how self-image works and is consistently speaking to your child in a way that raises it. The second expert, your child, has a challenge we all have: to control their self-talk. That's not easy for any of us. We are often our own worst critic. It takes practice to lock in the words and feelings that will propel us toward our potential. As a parent, you must exercise considerable discipline in expressing your feelings because if your child considers you an expert in swimming (even if they do not show it), your words matter greatly to them. What you say can push your child's self-image up or bring it crashing down.

One of the most valuable life lessons your child can learn in their competitive swimming experience is how to control their self-talk. You will get a glimpse of their self-talk when you overhear their expressions of emotions. Nearly all of us have, at one time or another, said to ourselves something along the lines of, "You stupid __" or "you idiot" or "dummy!" A poorly exercised action results in either blaming or learning. Focusing on what is to be *learned* from an action rather than *blaming* themselves or others is critical in the management of your child's self-image. The more your child focuses on learning rather than placing blame, the stronger their self-image will grow.

Good coaches understand the concept of raising self-image. They know to channel their critique with positive comments about what a swimmer is capable of. For example, if your child is going to practice, working both smart and hard, yet has a poor performance in a race, a coach who understands the value of increasing self-image might say, "Your efforts in practice have been like putting money in the bank. You didn't make a withdrawal today, but someday you will. Your investment is alive and well. The results are coming, just not today. You need more time to adapt to the work you're putting in."

One of the pitfalls for any swimmer and their parents is seeing a teammate who doesn't attend practice or work as hard swim really fast. If you compare your child or your child compares themself to that individual, it is like quicksand: comparison is a deadly habit to develop in your child's swimming career. The world is not fair in all ways or in all subjects. Some people are blessed with a beautiful singing voice, or height that enhances their talent and ability to play basketball. Others have a biological gift to swim fast. But the basic principle that the more work you put into something, the more you get out of it holds true in swimming. Focus on your child's best times and improving them.

Most swimmers, especially when they are young, see their parents as *experts*. Even though they might not want to admit it, they are watching and listening to your reactions to their ups and downs in the sport. Every word you say has consequences.

All parents make mistakes with the words they choose or the physical reaction they display in front of their children. Fortunately, the formation of our children's attitudes and the self-image that follows is not based on a single comment or even a few of them. Their attitudes and self-image are based on the predominance of input they receive from those they consider experts and the emotion (self-esteem) they feel when absorbing that input. Thus, a mistaken statement or action by Mom or Dad may be overcome by several more positive ones.

To be a great swimming parent, you need to do your best to protect and nurture your child's self-image. However, this *does not* mean that you should attempt to keep them from having difficult experiences. It *does* mean you need to help them learn from their disappointments and redirect their focus to the positive pictures that are associated with success.

Kelly Harrigan became an international champion for the United States, but her swimming career did not start that way. After one of her first races, when she was eight years old, the official told her, "You're DQ'd," indicating she had been disqualified. Kelly went to her mom and asked what DQ'd meant. Sue Harrigan said, "It means we're going to Dairy Queen!"

Yes, Kelly needed to learn how to swim her race correctly. Her coaches would help her with that at practice. Her mom turned young Kelly's attention to the joy of being at a swim meet. Dr. Kelly Harrigan (DVM) swam competitively through college and beyond and loves the sport so much that she trains and regularly competes in masters swimming today.

Like Kelly's mom, you can put your child's disappointment into perspective by facilitating joyful experiences. You're not ignoring their disappointment or misstep, just helping them get past it.

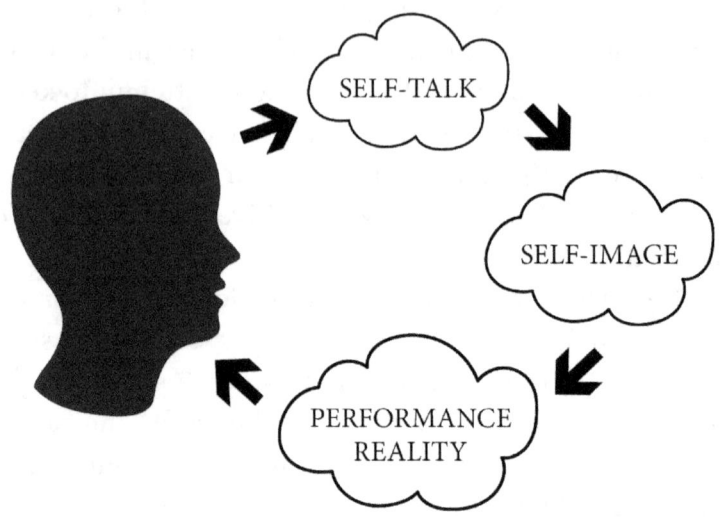

Each of us experiences a *self-image cycle*. This happens when words trigger pictures that bring about emotions that affect our performance. After a performance, self-talk, and words from those we consider experts start the cycle over again: words triggering pictures, leading to emotions. If the expert's words are positive, it is likely the next experience will also be positive or be a self-fulfilling prophecy. Unfortunately, if the dominant input after your child's performance is negative, this can also lead to a self-fulfilling prophecy, but one that is disappointing.

As your child progresses in swimming, good coaches will introduce the concept of goal visualization. In the self-image cycle, visualizations can replace the reality of a performance. One of the primary tools of any good athlete is to practice visualizing goals that are associated with performing at a particular capacity to raise their self-esteem. By vividly imagining an experience, athletes can improve their self-image and the corresponding comfort zone needed to perform at their optimum. Visualizing is a fun and powerful tool for everyone in anything they do. Sports are a training ground for this skill, which your child may use one day to argue a case in court, perform surgery, or have an important talk with their child.

The actress Katherine Hepburn was an early leader in women's rights. As an adult, Ms. Hepburn was fearless in confronting social or professional norms that characterized the middle of the twentieth century. Hepburn was once photographed, in her adolescence, standing on a tree limb high above the ground. The caption quoted her, "My parents never made me afraid."

Since your child was born, you have been giving them subtle feedback that has contributed greatly to shaping their self-image in many areas. Many parents are not as astute as Steve Jobs's parents or Sue Harrigan were when their children were just starting grade school. The younger your child, the easier it will be to elevate your subtle feedback to them and their self-image. If they are already in their teen years, they are likely to accept the sincerity of your comments more slowly. You may be getting a late start, but be patient and persistent in helping your child improve their self-image. It's never too late to become a great swimming parent. Here are a few phrases that might come in handy at some point:

- When you swim fast, you'll remember this as a stepping stone you learned from.
- Do you know what Thomas Edison said after he failed on his ten-thousandth attempt to find a

filament to create the electric light bulb? He said, with a smile, "I have not failed. I've just found ten thousand ways that won't work."

- Honey, I wish I could swim like you can. It's amazing to me what you've already accomplished in the sport. I love watching your effort to get to practice, how you listen to your coach, and your determination to improve.

- You know what Taylor Swift says, "Anything you put your mind to and your imagination into can make your life a lot better and a lot more fun."

- You know what else she says? "I think *fearless* is having fears but jumping anyway."

- You know what Michael Jordan says, "Success isn't something you chase. It's something you have to put forth the effort for constantly. Then maybe it'll come when you least expect it. Most people don't understand that."

Hard Work

Competitive swimming is a blue collar sport in which *work works*. To achieve their potential, your child will have to go to practice and work hard. Who do you know that works hard at something they are convinced they cannot be successful at?

Hard work in a pursuit comes naturally to people who have a high self-image in that activity. Once children begin to see themselves succeeding, more hard work will follow. Be ready to facilitate and aid this effort by getting them to practices and swim meets. As they move into their teen years, plan your family vacations and other commitments to allow them to execute the consistent hard work they will need to realize their potential. Family vacations during the training season will most certainly diminish your child's efforts toward reaching their potential. The older your swimmer gets, the more important this becomes.

Personal Responsibility

Brian Goodell was not a big boy with exceptional swimming talent. Until he was a teenager, he loved playing tackle football in addition to being a competitive swimmer. When Brian gave up football to dedicate himself to becoming the best swimmer he could be, he agreed to attend swim practice early in the morning and after school. His mother, Reba Goodell, arranged a carpool to help her with the early morning trips to the pool. All too frequently, however, Brian didn't want to get out of bed and go. Reba thought about how to approach the problem with her son.

"Brian, I've canceled the carpool," she told her thirteen-year-old son. "When you want to go to practice in the morning, you wake me up, and I'll drive you. If you miss practice and your coach calls, you get to talk with him."

Reba Goodell instinctively knew that for Brian to succeed in his sport, he would have to take personal responsibility for his success. When Brian was seventeen years old, he won two gold medals at the Montreal Olympics, both in world record time. Then, he entered his senior year of high school.

Most children start by swimming for their mom and dad. By *swimming for* I mean that Mom and Dad's approval is the primary source of their motivation to attend practice, race at meets, and succeed. Most children then transfer their source of motivation from their parents to their coach, but the most successful swimmers get to the point where they swim for themselves. In other words, they accept personal responsibility for their motivation and development in the sport. When Brian's mom turned the responsibility for his swimming over to her son, Brian accepted it and thrived.

Tim Shaw was a good age-group swimmer but was mischievous and often played around at practice during his preteen years. In those early years, Tim watched his father pressure his older brother about attending practice and working hard. When Tim turned thirteen years old, he made up his mind that he wanted to see how good a swimmer he could be. But, at the dinner table one night, he announced a stipulation for his parents: "I'm going to start working hard and see how good I can get, but I have a condition," he told his mom and dad. "I don't want you to come to my swim practices or meets."

His parents agreed.

About three years after Tim's parents subscribed to Tim's plan to accept personal responsibility for his swimming success or failure, he set three world records at the national championships. His parents were at home, a four-hour drive away, during what was a historic performance. Years later, as I chronicled Tim's career in the book *Four Champions, One Gold Medal*, Tim's mother told me, "The greatest thing we did was let the sport be Tim's."

A strong argument can be made that Katie Ledecky is the greatest female swimmer in history. At this writing, Katie is favored to compete in Paris at her fourth Olympics. Her love of working hard for so many years is rare in the sport. It's especially unusual, as Katie moves into her late twenties, to be at the top of the world in the distance races.

Where does that love of training come from?

When Katie was ten years old, her coach, Carolyn Kaucher, would occasionally ask her to write out her own training set and then perform it successfully. Katie learned at a very young age to take personal responsibility for her swimming and to find joy in working hard at practice.

Out of Body Experience

The pinnacle of sports performance can be a *spiritual* or out-of-body experience. In 1986 Bill Moyers was putting together his monumental PBS series entitled "The Power of Myth" with world renown expert in mythology and spirituality, Joseph Campbell. Moyers asked Campbell, whose work inspired the *Star Wars* movie empire, what his most perfect experience was in life. Campbell, then in his eighties, thought for a moment. "When I was running track at Columbia." He went on to describe a particular day and how perfect his performance was, individually and on a relay. Campbell's description was of an "invisible force that was propelling him forward."

To master any physical activity takes hundreds, if not thousands of hours of practice. The final step to reaching one's potential is not a physical one. It comes from visualizations or an invisible perfecting of the skills, pace, rhythm, and effort required to perform as perfectly as possible.

As noted earlier, in 1977, Brian Goodell was the last male under six feet tall to set a world record in freestyle. Brian used what one might describe as *energizations*: he consistently practiced visualizing extraordinary performances that included an energy component. Brian visualized himself finishing a long race in which he was the pilot of a 747 airplane. In Brian's mind, his tired body mimicked the wings that were madly vibrating and shaking while his internal engine roared to propel him forward. Meanwhile, Brian was under full control in the pilot's seat, landing the plane and finishing his race.

A great swimming parent will not be in the middle of their child's visualizations or energizations. But know that if your child is going to become a champion swimmer, they will be exploring this dynamic tool.

"Oh, I'm not concerned about my child becoming a champion," you say. Perhaps if you could define *champion* differently, you would be. A winning time in almost any race would lose in another race. Winning is about circumstance. Our definition of a champion, therefore, is a person who does everything they can to be the fastest swimmer they can be by executing each step of the aforementioned pyramid to the best of their ability.

If your child has two great swimming parents, the process is made possible.

CHAPTER 4

Social Media

"Social media has given us this idea that we should all have a posse of friends, [when in reality], if we have one or two really good friends, we are lucky."

—Brene Brown

It is important for the great swim parent to decide how to manage the unique effects that social media has on our kids today, whether to positively affect their child's swimming or to simply safeguard their child's personal development. This topic could have been touched upon in the previous sections on delayed gratification or self-image because those two important qualities needed in a successful swimmer can be intertwined with habits surrounding your child's engagement with social media. There are many other resources for you to deeply explore your options for managing this difficult subject. We're only going to touch upon it briefly.

Most parents today grew up experiencing the effects of television and computer screens. We should know that a basic tenet of early childhood development is that children under the age of twenty-four months should seldom be in front of any screen—TV, computer, or phone. The reason is that if they see life through a screen, they tend to think there is magic living outside the self rather than learning at a young age that splendor, wonder, and contentment come from inside. When we learn at a young age to entertain ourselves with our imagination, the experience allows for infinite exploration, creative development, and the sense that there is greatness *inside of us.*

The advent of social media raised the stakes even higher because every parent must navigate how to allow for its benefits while protecting their child from huge negatives. For example, a phone can help with safety and communication. Among the negatives, however, are when people post videos on a screen that may make them appear to have it *all figured out.* This poses to the child (or even a parent) the question, "Why don't I have it all together?"

That phone or computer app produces texts, likes, and swift responses. Each text or like triggers a chemical in the brain called dopamine, which feels good! Like alcohol, nicotine, and other chemicals, dopamine is highly addictive. While we have age restrictions for the use of alcohol and nicotine, there are no age restrictions on social media use unless parents establish them.

A teen's struggle with adolescence encourages them to look for soothing experiences. Almost every alcoholic discovered alcohol as a teenager. When stress comes, a teenager can turn to the bottle, and this can become addictive. I sadly recall what one of my peers said just before dying of liver cancer from alcoholism: "I just can't stop drinking." The habit had started in his teen years.

The trauma kids experience over whether they have enough friends, likes, or people following them is something we parents haven't dealt with before. Social media friendships do not have the deep connection that enables friends to share problems and questions they encounter in their lives. Many kids live in fear that they will be ridiculed or *canceled* if they do or say the wrong thing. There is seldom any arguing, discussing, or face-to-face negotiation. They are either *in* or abruptly *out* of a social-media-based relationship.

When someone sits at dinner with their phone out, texting people who are not there, that is an addiction. They are not experiencing the deep meaning that can come in a conversation with those right there in front of them. Their mind is jumping to whatever stimulant of the moment arrives, looking for the next text and hit of dopamine. Social behaviors of this nature also send a message to those at the table that they just are not that important.

We now have a generation of children laced with impatience. Gone are the days of waiting to see next week's edition of a favorite TV show. We can binge TV shows from start to finish. We start the day with a text (and dopamine hit). Amazon offers us sameday delivery for whatever we need. However, Amazon cannot deliver meaningful relationships and a sense of self-worth.

Today, many children struggle to develop coping mechanisms to deal with stress. Studies show higher percentages of our youth now have low self-esteem compared to in years past. Strong, rich relationships come from difficult, messy, uncomfortable processes. Things that really matter require time and patience. The same applies to swimming, where success requires delayed gratification and progressive returns on work investment.

To be a great swim parent or simply a great parent, you need to confront and tackle the social media phenomenon and put it in its proper place.

CHAPTER 5

Theory of Desirable Difficulty

"When everything seems to be going against you, remember that the airplane takes off against the wind, not with it."

—Henry Ford

In 1994, UCLA psychologist Dr. Robert Bjork introduced the concept of *desirable difficulty*. Bjork's research showed something you may already know: when learning, we retain more when we figure out the answer to a problem than we do when we're simply told what the answer is. To lead a student through desirable difficulty is to challenge that student to think. This can be stressful and difficult at times. Bjork's research applied the phrase *challenge point* to that key moment in the learning process that strains the student.

Learning challenges should be progressive over a child's life. When teaching three-year-old children to swim, there are challenge points that teachers must confront and take advantage of to help the child learn to put their face in the water and eventually learn to float and swim. Good coaching in the sport of competitive swimming progresses from gentle challenges for seven- and eight-year-olds to gradual increases in intensity over the next several years. A young athlete in their teens should be able to accept formidable challenges.

When your child pursues the larger goal of finding out how fast they can swim, they learn to make smaller goals for that season, broken down into weekly and even daily goals. A coach's role in helping your child achieve those goals is to tell your child the truth about their efforts, performance, and results. It won't always be easy for your child to hear that they need to improve their skills, their pacing, their concentration, or other techniques. Nor will it always be comfortable for your swimmer to honestly examine their overall effort in practice or in racing. When a qualified, well-intentioned coach, with an eye on progress, challenges their swimmers by addressing the performance, not the person, it's not abuse; it's good coaching.

Before David Boies became one of the premier trial attorneys in the United States, he was a struggling student at the University of Redlands. The university is a small school in Southern California with strong requirements for reading in undergraduate coursework. Boies struggled terribly in academics because he was severely dyslexic. He couldn't read the material needed to get through the coursework to graduate. This challenge caused him to become a great listener.

By the time Boies had graduated from Yale Law School, he had honed his ability to listen intently in lectures. Eventually, his ability to keenly absorb a witness's testimony in the courtroom became his strength. It was the skill of *listening* that earned him recognition as a latter-day Clarence Darrow for his brilliant work in very high-profile cases. Still working in his 80s, he most recently represented victims abused by Jeffrey Epstein.

Parents often overestimate their control of their children and underestimate their children's ability to find a way to succeed and their capacity for tenacity. Some parents mistakenly feel that they need to protect, prompt, and push their children in order for them to succeed in swimming and in life.

The list below is of notable (sometimes notorious) people who lost one of their parents at an early age (their age at the time and which parent are in parentheses).

Lost a Parent and Ruled the World

- Napoleon Bonaparte (father, 15)
- George Washington (father, 11)
- Thomas Jefferson (father, 14)
- Abraham Lincoln (mother, 9)
- Vladimir Lenin (father, 15)
- Adolf Hitler (father, 13)
- Mahatma Gandhi (father, 15)
- Joseph Stalin (father, 11)
- Bill Clinton (father, infant)
- Michelangelo (mother, 6)
- Ralph Waldo Emerson (father, 8)
- Herman Melville (father, 12)
- Friedrich Nietzsche (father, 4)

- Mark Twain (father, 11)
- Steve Allen (father, 1)
- Tim Allen (father, 11)
- Lucille Ball (father, 3)
- Steven Colbert (father, 6)
- Billy Crystal (father, 15)
- Eddie Murphy (father, 8)
- Rosie O'Donnell (father, 11)
- Red Skelton (father, infant)
- Tom and Dick Smothers (father, 7 & 8)
- Paul McCartney (mother, 14)
- John Lennon (mother, 17)

Although the pain of losing a parent is enormous, it also unleashes a resourcefulness in a child that is prompted by the instinct to accept more responsibility in one's life. When a swim parent steps back and allows their swimmer to work with their coach to unbridle their powers in swimming, it is amazing how much progress they can make. They are allowing their child to partner with the coach on a shared journey that will test their limits and enable them to achieve more than the parent or child thought possible. The swimmers will learn their lessons in a more effective way when they struggle in this process.

When your child takes ownership of their swimming progress, they will improve at a much faster rate. To be a great swimming parent, you must let go of trying to coach swimming and rather focus your attention on teaching them the core life skills of respect, integrity, and effort. Often, these skills are best taught in emotional moments when your child is filled with disappointment. These are the challenge points for a parent aspiring to reach their highest potential to be at their loving best.

One of the most important contributions a parent can give to their schoolage child is to provide them the opportunity to be mentored by good teachers and good coaches. Sit back and watch them work to become a faster swimmer and a hard worker. Praise not only their effort to improve themselves but also to help their team so they will learn how to support and work with others in and out of the pool.

When your son or daughter faces a demanding situation, think back to when you faced a difficult circumstance in your life that produced a valuable lesson. Allow your child to have the same opportunity as you did to encounter that "desirable difficulty." The cliché "Prepare the child for the path, not the path for the child" earned its repeated utterance because of its fundamental wisdom in knowing that eventually neither mom or dad will be around to make your child's critical decisions and provide the fortitude to see them through.

CHAPTER 6

Create Opportunities, Not Obligations

*"Not all of us can do great things.
But we can do small things with great love."*
—Mother Teresa

When I coached the Cincinnati Pepsi Marlins back in the 1980s, there was a family on our team named Rhodenbaugh. They were one of the great swimming families in American history. Three of their eight children became an Olympic Trial finalist, an NCAA Champion (and World University Games gold medalist), and an Olympian. But that was after their dad learned a key lesson speaking to his oldest, who never achieved that level of success.

Dr. Rhodenbaugh told me a story that I often asked him to relate to our parents. His oldest son was racing in a summer club meet. Dad came hustling in from his medical practice to see the meet. His son narrowly missed winning one of his very first races. When his father greeted him after the race, he said excitedly, "Son, you were THIS close to winning that race! Why didn't you go a little faster?" His son, suddenly teary-eyed, looked up at his dad and said, "I did the best I could."

Dr. Rhodenbaugh saw the hurt in his son's eyes and realized that his response caused his son's disappointment. He learned quickly to praise the *effort*, not the outcome of his children's endeavors.

When effort is praised in swimming, in school, or in other activities, a parent can create a repeatable possibility or *opportunity* for their child to realize. When a parent judges their child's performance by their *outcome*, even when it is an outstanding one, they are creating an *obligation*: to swim another fast time, to win a race, or to get another A in school. That outcome isn't always going to be repeatable because no swimmer always swims a new best time, no swimmer wins every race, and almost no student gets an A in every class. However, the *effort* to prepare and do one's best *is* repeatable each time. Eventually, this becomes a habit, and great results will follow for your child.

In the long run, it will be the effort that will determine your child's personal satisfaction in how they engage the world. The two most important experts in their life—their parents—teach them to focus on trying their hardest when they are a child. When parents use their child's effort as the measuring stick, their girl or boy has the best chance to succeed in the pool and beyond.

CHAPTER 7

Coach Life, Not Swimming

"When I was a boy of fourteen, my father was so ignorant I could hardly stand to have the old man around. But when I got to be twenty-one, I was astonished at how much the old man had learned in seven years."

—Mark Twain

Swim teams hire coaches instead of parents for a reason: whether good or bad at what they do, every coach has more experience in competitive swimming than the parents do. In those rare cases when the parent has more expertise in the sport than the coach, it is especially difficult to avoid the temptation to be a *backseat* coach. In this situation, one good option is to join the coaching staff. Give your time and expertise to *all* the team members, which also sets a great example of community service for your child. But if you do join the staff, be sure you turn back into Mom or Dad when leaving the pool.

If you choose to be a backseat coach, chances are your child will lose confidence in their actual swim coach, which can be devasting to your child's experience in the sport. Overstated? No. The ugly alternative is that your child sides with the coach, and you become an annoyance, and your child does not want to hear anything you have to say about swimming.

Trust in one's coach is essential if your child is going to reach their potential. Thus, backseat coaching or questioning your child's coach in front of your swimmer will erode their trust in the coach. This behavior is one of the most harmful mistakes a swimming parent can make.

Your child is best served if you stick to coaching *life*. There is a lot to work on there. Being on time is a good place to start. It shows respect and consideration for other people's time. They must also learn to show respect to their competitors, coaches, and officials. Their coach may address this, but if not, make sure your child treats others by your standards and expectations.

Matt Biondi won nine gold medals collectively in the 1984, 1988, and 1992 Olympics. While watching professional tennis matches on TV, Matt saw temper tantrums, with players slamming rackets and yelling at line judges and other unacceptable behavior. One day, when he was twelve, he reproduced similar unsportsmanlike behavior during a match. Abruptly, he felt his mother pulling him off the court by his ear. Without a word, she put him in her car and drove him home. Matt's mother never scolded him, but he got the message: "That is not the way the Biondis conduct themselves." Matt not only achieved enormous success as a swimmer, but he also grew up to be a wonderful, respectful man.

Dealing with disappointment should be high on every parent's list of life lessons to teach their child. Throwing goggles or exhibiting temper tantrums is an area that, if not addressed by your child's coach, should be by you.

Look for other life skills that your child can improve through swimming. Are they a good teammate? Do they show interest when their friends and teammates swim? You can't push your swimmer to show an interest in their younger teammates, but being a role model to younger members of the team has multiple benefits. Your child will improve their leadership skills, the younger swimmers will improve faster, and so will the team.

A subtle approach that works well is to look for opportunities to "catch your child doing something right." A comment on the car ride home like, "I'll bet that little guy really appreciated your interest in him," will encourage your child to repeat the behavior. Hopefully, you'll also have the opportunity to comment favorably on the way they congratulated a competitor, cheered for a teammate, put lots of effort into a race, showed empathy in consoling a teammate, picked up their trash, thanked their coach, and other qualities that you want to see your child develop.

Teach your child to learn all they can from their coach by encouraging them to *listen* to their coach. Telling your son or daughter anecdotes about your background or encounters or about someone they respect is a great way to strengthen the connection with your child. The younger they are, the more likely they will welcome your experiences and thoughts.

As they get started, you might try to gently suggest that they look their coach in the eye when they are talking with them. That is a great habit to develop. Once they have taken a moment to process what they've been told, encourage them to say, "Got it, coach!" Coaches have loads of expertise to offer their swimmers and tend to embrace a good listener's eagerness by sharing more of their wisdom. Any swimmer who actively listens to their coach is sure to get more coaching.

As for your coaching? Remember, this sports experience is going to end at some point. Keep looking for opportunities to coach life, just like Matt Biondi's mom did. The sport of swimming should stay in its proper perspective: a sampling of how your loved one is going to handle their life experiences to come.

CHAPTER 8

Parenting Is a Contact Sport

"Tell me and I forget. Teach me and I remember. Involve me and I learn."

—BENJAMIN FRANKLIN

John Davis was one of the most celebrated and accomplished swimmers in the history of the University of North Carolina. Full disclosure: I was privileged to coach John during his age-group years and again during his summers home from college. Today, John is a counselor for wayward teenage boys. He chronicles some of his experiences and methodology in his book *Extreme Pursuit: Winning the Race for the Heart of Your Son.*

The boys that John counsels are generally addicted to drugs, alcohol, crime, or all three. He explains the characteristics of fathers that lead teenagers to this point:

- Fathers who are very successful in their work life
- Dads who have very high expectations for their sons
- Dads who have little time to spend with their boys and when they do, they are critical of them

The work John does to help "his boys" is unusual but very effective. It often includes major mountaineering experiences. Climbing mountains is not something most parents are ready for, but there are two bits of advice that John offers that every parent can use.

First, John notes that *parenting is a contact sport.* In your child's early years, being physically engaged in their activities is a very important part of their development. As they get older, being present and engaged is still important, but it can be made more difficult in our children's teen years when they may not want us around as much as they used to. Carve out time to be with them. Even being their chauffeur is an important time together. They can't run from the conversation when you're driving them to practice!

One-on-one trips or traditions with a parent can not only generate wonderful memories but can also produce critical opportunities for you to listen to your child. Verbal prompts, followed by long bouts of listening, can keep you abreast of your child's feelings, challenges, obstacles, and opportunities they are confronting. Former presidential candidate Mitt Romney held family meetings with the lights out so his five boys could say what was on their minds without fear of their parents' visual responses.

Second, John says that *shoulder-to-shoulder experience* is key to growing your child's self-respect. John recommends treating your child's view as being equally important to your own. Try to see the world through your child's eyes before sharing your view. For example, some parents are quick to tell their children their opinion first on everything from politics to the environment to sports or to the best music ever made. Learn your child's perspective by listening to them first. Show your child respect through shoulder-to-shoulder experiences, and it will teach them to articulate their own opinion and value it.

Perhaps you're anxious to get the wisdom that is in your mind into your child's? And do it quickly? One of John's high school teammates was Sean Kelly. Sean went on to become a philosophy professor, and at this writing, is the Dean of Arts and Humanities at Harvard College. Sean says that when he began teaching, he thought his responsibility was to provide the greatest ninety-minute lecture he could. This included eloquent historical references to key philosophical scholars then tying them back into present-day theory and practice. Eventually, Sean had an epiphany he was lecturing, not teaching.

Professor Kelly changed his approach. He started asking students what they were studying, and his classes came alive. Sean, a scholar and New York Times Best-Selling author, began to have students join him in shoulder-to-shoulder experiences about philosophy. As his students became engaged, learning accelerated.

Once you position yourself shoulder to shoulder with your child in life, the journey with them will get richer and deeper for both of you. They may also open up more about how they are feeling about their experience in swimming, giving you the chance to show your love and support for them more broadly.

CHAPTER 9

Don't Sell Your Kid Short

"Sometimes you may feel you're raising an alien, and sometimes your child will feel like they are being raised by one."

—Anonymous

Gillian Lynne was born in Great Britain. Gillian struggled so much in school that when she was thirteen years old, her frustrated mother took her to a doctor for help. Her mother wanted to find a way for Gillian to sit still in school, focus, learn, and prepare for a career. The doctor sat and listened patiently to the mother and Gillian. Then he told Gillian he needed to speak privately with her mother. Before they left the room, the doctor turned on the radio. The doctor and mother peeked in at Gillian to see what she was doing when left alone. She was dancing.

The doctor convinced Gillian's mother to support Gillian and *her* passion. Gillian carved out a long career in dance, including choreographing two of the longest-running shows on Broadway: *Cats* and *Phantom of the Opera*. She also became a television and film star. Gillian's spectacular career included receiving many prestigious accolades. In 2018, the New London Theatre was renamed the Gillian Lynne Theatre, making it the only theatre in London's famed

West End named after anyone but a Royal.

Michael Phelps struggled in school because it was hard for him to sit still. Drugs were prescribed to help him focus. He did not like the drugs, and in seventh grade, he asked his mother to get him off the medication. Ms. Phelps, a middle school principal and single mom, listened to her son. She agreed to a gradual reduction and then elimination of the meds. Michael replaced the medication with gobs of training in the pool that helped him swim faster and faster.

As we know, Michael Phelps went on to swim in five Olympics, winning twenty-three gold medals, the most of any athlete in history. His net worth today is estimated at 100 million dollars.

Neither Gillian nor Michael fit their parents' initial expectations for behavior and academic success. Nonetheless, their parents supported them in pursuing their passions. The result has not only been business success and fame but true personal fulfillment for each of them.

Each of our children has something wonderful to offer the world. Someone has to choreograph Broadway shows, and there has to be an Olympic champion. Why not your child? Don't ever sell them short. Get out of their way so you can see what they can do in the field they are most passionate about.

CHAPTER 10

Beware of Destination Disease

"Put her to sleep yourself every night. Sing to her and cradle her in your arms. And sit by her side every night. Because one day you won't be able to, and it's going to happen really fast."

—Salma Hayek

Parenting isn't easy. You may have initially felt many difficult moments during your child's *terrible twos*. If they have reached their teen years, you have surely felt them again. At times, you might want to crawl in a hole or take a sustained break while these rough parenting periods pass. Finding time to reconnect to your spiritual center and review your values for your family is important, but beware! Beware of *destination disease*.

Destination disease is when a parent retreats for hours, days, or longer, believing that, eventually, these tough times will pass. It is tempting to think that by avoiding interaction with your child, they will figure it out on their own, and all will be healed in your relationship. Believing that one day you'll be watching your smiling child walk through high school or college graduation, a glorious wedding day, or other milestones in their life without your best efforts each day is succumbing to destination disease. You have taken the time to read this book, which shows how much you care about avoiding that pitfall.

Success each day as a parent starts with the self-awareness that requires quiet moments of reflection. Perhaps your method is meditation, journaling, prayer, running or swimming, or another similar activity. Once you are centered, engage. When your child's emotions are at their peak, it is important that you stay calm. Listen to what your child is saying. Cut through their emotion while containing yours. Get to the heart of the matter. Respond surgically, logically, and most importantly, lovingly.

I was at a summer swim meet and witnessed this family interaction: A thirteen-year-old girl was swimming the one-hundred-yard butterfly for the first time. The distance was a big step up from the fifty-yard lengths the young lady was used to swimming in the eleven to twelve age group. The girl started fast, then fell apart. In the last length, she could hardly get her arms out of the water. She exited the pool in enormous pain, trudged a few steps toward her mother and father, and then had an emotional breakdown that included a flood of tears. Her mother hugged her and simultaneously yelled at the girl's dad. "This is supposed to be fun, and it isn't," she screamed in his direction. "You are able to fix this [talk with the coaches] and you better do it!"

Then something happened that surprised me. The girl stopped crying, raised her voice, and said, "Mom, shut up!" Those were not words she commonly used in addressing her mother. She appreciated her mother's embrace, but she wasn't asking anyone to fix the situation or heal her pain. No one was injured or harmed. The young lady just wanted to be loved and supported in that moment of athletic distress, a miserable moment that every athlete eventually experiences.

In Daniel Goleman's brilliant book *Emotional Intelligence: Why It Can Matter More Than IQ* , he examines the emotions we have as parents, which have a huge impact on our effectiveness. Consider Goleman's theory and how it fits this difficult exchange between this girl and her parents.

Goleman suggests that there are three kinds of empathy that are critical to parenting. The first is *cognitive empathy*. This is our ability to objectively put ourselves in our child's shoes. Their pain might trigger the recollection of a moment in our childhood that we can draw on. From this perspective, one can formulate words to express our understanding of how our child feels.

Secondly, Goleman submits that the brain has a specific capacity for *social empathy*. This is connecting the emotions in yourself to what another is feeling. For example, you know what it feels like to invest time and effort into succeeding at something. You know how disappointing it feels when your expectations are not met and how exhilarating it feels when they are. As a swimmer, your child will have this experience too. Their improvement will have ups, and it will have downs. You can develop a rapport with your swimmer so they know you feel their pain. From this position, they will grow their trust in you and their connection to you.

Finally, Goleman uses the term *empathetic concern*. This can be described as the love that a person has for their child, a friend, or a neighbor and their desire to help. For nearly all parents, this maternal instinct is easily triggered. The girl felt that love from her mom and visibly appreciated her mother's strong hug.

Goleman argues that all three types of empathy are required for good relationships and to be an effective parent.

Absent from the mother's reaction to her daughter's experience was an objective, cognitive response. Sometimes, as a parent, it is best to say nothing until the cognitive connections can be made and one makes their best effort to find the right words to match the moment. The emotional outburst by the mother clearly did nothing to comfort her daughter. The mom had, in fact, had a long, successful competitive swimming career. Had she been able to center and calm herself, she might have added to her welcomed hug gentle words such as, "Oh honey, I remember my first one-hundred-yard butterfly and how much it hurt."

These moments are much easier to analyze after the fact than execute in realtime, but that is why you are reading this book—to learn from the mistakes of others to avoid reacting and improve how you respond. If that well-intentioned mother could have provided those gentle words that connected her own feelings with those of her daughters, they would have heightened the rapport between the two of them.

What happened after that difficult swim?

The young lady's coaches entered her in the one-hundred-yard butterfly a week later! She learned to pace herself in the first part of the race. She improved her best time by six seconds in one week and climbed from the pool bubbling with self-esteem and a smile. Proud coaches and parents greeted her.

As you execute your own empathetic management, you will be teaching your child to have a higher emotional quotient. For example, when we forgive our children, we teach *them* to forgive. If you have established a healthy rapport with your child, no matter what the challenge or conflict, they will come back to you. They become great kids because of the understanding, loving, and supportive environment you have created in your family.

By intending to become a great swim parent, you can simultaneously strive to be the very best parent you can be. We all recall mistakes and wonderful moments that our parents executed in raising us. Draw on your own childhood experiences, consider the information from this book, commit to objective analysis of your behavior, and you can take a large step forward in serving your youngster.

Where is your child, what are they doing, and how can you use what you have learned to tweak your parenting?

Create new habits and do it now. Start small, then repeat and build on your loving, supportive behavior. It is *their* life; embrace *their* healthy passions. They are, in fact, small, unique people that one day may grow to parent your grandchildren. Modeling what you want your child to become has enormous power. Strive to set an example in your behavior, emotions, and word choices every day.

Hard work? You can look at it that way. A different perspective is that it is the honor of your lifetime to shed light and love all over your loved one.

Their journey as an athlete will be a microcosm of their life's journey, giving them the opportunity to grow in a safer setting than they would have had if they had not become committed to their potential in a sport. You can help your child elevate their swimming, change their life, and ultimately change their world for the better. As the years go by, your child will look back with increasing perspective on your empathy and support and appreciate you as a *great swimming parent*!

Epilogue

The parenting landscape is a dynamic one. Our ancestors traversed a society once based on agriculture to a one-hundred-year process of industrialization (1865-1965) and into the digital/information age. Now we embark on a culture that includes artificial intelligence. The great swim parent must adjust to those vicissitudes, while manifesting the fundamental truths expressed in these pages.

One large change in the last twenty years is the development of the internet and the quick access to the information that it offers. Having information is often confused with being informed. The latter requires long study and perspective derived from experience that leads to wisdom. A parent drawing information from the internet about how their child's training in swimming should be conducted can be a problem today that wasn't present twenty-five years ago. Pursuing expert guidance for your child's technical experience in swimming in this way is a mistake.

There have always been different ways to train to swim fast. Some coaches opt for more endurance training and others use more speed work to develop their swimmers. That big picture hasn't changed in at least fifty years. There are various approaches to a swimmer's development of conditioning that can work. If you have questions in this area, they should be directed to the coach and outpace the conclusions you might draw from bits and pieces of information you acquire.

In the long run, it is going to be your life coaching that will most benefit your child.

Consider this story from Coach George Block's squad in San Antonio, Texas. There was a boy that was so slow on his swim team that when there was a distance race the boy would often be swimming in the opposite direction of his competitors on the final length or lengths. In practice, he was often swimming behind his teammates, also in the opposite direction. Thus, he earned the nickname "Wrong Way." After high school, "Wrong Way" enlisted in the military and was assigned duty on a vessel. His boat encountered terrible sea conditions, washing overboard some of the service men. Wrong Way's swimming skill was far greater than any of the other seaman. He plunged into the water, saving the lives of service person, after service person, a feat no other on his vessel could accomplish.

You may not see the fruits of being a great swim parent quickly. You may need to exhibit your own delayed gratification. In addition to all the benefits of emotional development, friendship acquisition, and physical prowess, it is possible that the skill and fortitude your child acquires as a competitive swimmer will save their own life. It is also likely they will save the life of another.

THE END

Acknowledgments

Twenty years of heartache, exhilaration, conflict, and resolution with the athletes and their parents at the Redlands Swim Club, Katy Aquatic Club, Wilton Y, Cincinnati Pepsi Marlins, and the Sarasota Y have created the lessons for this book. I'm grateful to each swimmer and parent for putting up with me during my process of attempting to develop the skills to effectively talk with parents about their child and their experiences in the sport of swimming.

It was my honor, during my college coaching years, to conduct the ARETE Swim Camp for twenty-four years. During that time my work with more than four thousand swimmers and their caring parents helped me put into words the path that the best swimming families take to experience all that the sport can give them.

The editorial support of Jeri Leer and Dana Abbott have been invaluable to creating what I hope is clarity for the content of this book. Patricia Marshall and her staff at Luminare Press have done such great work again for me. Thank you to Luminare's Kim Harper-Kennedy, Kristen Brack, and Sallie Vandagrift who have been so patient and thorough in their expertise.

Finally, being the father of Annie Warner has been the greatest honor a person could have. The lessons from helping Annie grow into an accomplished, kind, young woman through her experiences in sports, dance, and teaching are the heart of this book. Just as we embrace the hearts of our kids in our hands, they do the same for us.

How To Be a Great Swim Parent
is also available as an audiobook.

Find it on:
BlackstoneLibrary.com

Questions and Answers

Should I allow my child to play other sports?
Yes! The best way for your child to find out if they want to apply themselves in any sport is to try several to see which one they like best. The younger they are when you do this the better; preferably when they are beginning elementary school. To excel in a sport today to be a strong contributor on a high school or college team, most children will need to be zeroing in on their main sport before they leave middle school.

In our home, we had a "rule" that our daughter was to play a sport each season. Our logic was that it was a part of her education, kept her busy in a productive way, and helped her make active friends. It was up to her to decide what sport or sports to play. She started with gymnastics, swimming, softball, and dance. She decided at about fourteen to commit to competitive dance, pretty much yearlong (and often close to twenty hours a week!) and continued to enjoy it in a team format through college.

Is it a good idea to enroll my swimmer in clinics or camps?
Clinics tend to be one- or two-day events that emphasize technique, starts, and turns. They can be inspiring if they include highly successful coaches and/or swimmers. They can be instructional if they are well thought out and the

coach to swimmer ratio is much better than your child's team training is.

Camps tend to be several days or weeks. They can also be inspiring, fun experiences that may help light the fire in your child to want to excel in swimming. However, if your swimmer is moving into their teen years and becoming an accomplished swimmer, taking time out from the consistent training with their own home coach may not be advised. If your son or daughter is in their teen years, it tends to be best to bow to the wishes of their coach of whether or not to attend a camp.

At our camp, the most highly enrolled age-group and gender were girls thirteen to fourteen years old. Many were struggling with whether or not to continue in swimming. A positive, enlightening camp experience tended to inspire them to do so.

Should I enroll my swimmer in private technique instruction?

The best swim teams will incorporate technique in practice every day. Good technique and skills can be compared to an artist sculpting a figure from marble. It takes a vision by the artist (coach) of the end result and then constant attention and commitment by coach and swimmer to work toward that end. If your child's primary coach is offering private instruction, it certainly would make sense to take advantage of it, if you can. But a completely separate coach might not have the same vision, especially if they aren't on the team's coaching staff.

There are many "technique coaches" available today that are not a part of the regular swim team. Although they can be good teachers, registering for private instruction with such a coach sends a message to your swimmer that they are not getting what they need from their regular swim team coach. That isn't good (see Chapter 2). It is likely they will lose trust in their coach.

A good practice is to ask your child's coach what they think about private instruction. If they support it, then it's important to have an open line of communication about what the team coach is teaching your swimmer and what the private coach is teaching your swimmer. You want to avoid your child having to cope with conflicting information.

What if my son or daughter wants to quit during the season?

First, try to avoid that situation. The best way to enter the sport of swimming tends to be to join a neighborhood team in a local summer swim league. The reasons are it's a short season (usually six to eight weeks), low on training, high on racing, and fun!! By starting in summer league, you can gauge your child's interest.

Once they join a team for the school year, they are likely committing to six months or more of practice and competition. That is a big commitment, especially when you first start the sport.

Quitting is not a step any parent welcomes. Unfortunately, it can become a habit. If it's your child's decision to join the team, we suggest doing everything you can to help them honor that commitment to finish the season. Then take a break. Then decide whether or not to continue.

About the Author

Chuck Warner has been a leader in competitive swimming for nearly fifty years through his coaching, writing, speaking, and service. In 2022, he became one of fewer than one hundred coaches in American history to be inducted into the American Swimming Coaches Hall of Fame.

Coach Warner has previously authored three highly acclaimed books on swimming: *Four Champions, One Gold Medal*; *...And Then They Won Gold: Stepping Stones to Swimming Excellence*; and *Eddie Reese: Coaching Swimming, Teaching Life*. He has also written more than fifty articles published by *Swimming World*, *USA Swimming*, *American Swimming Magazine*, and *Swim Swam*.

Other Books by Chuck Warner

A look inside the heart, mind, training steps, and spirit of eight athletes that collectively won twenty-eight Olympic Gold Medals: Dave Berkoff, Matt Biondi, Ian Crocker, Josh Davis, Mike Barrowman, Lenny Krayzelburg, Grant Hackett, and Aaron Piersol.

"With his latest book…*And Then They Won Gold*, coach and author Chuck Warner solidifies his position as the John C. Maxwell and Malcom Gladwell of Swimming, by explaining success and emphasizing the importance of the idea that Talent alone is never enough."

—Bruce Wigo, Chief Executive Officer,
International Swimming Hall of Fame

Available at Amazon and WWW.CHUCKWARNERBOOKS.COM

"There are few times in a life when one is humbled by an exhibition of life and of its depiction. This is one. This book is a must-read, not simply for those in the aquatic world, but for every human being searching for a compass in life and a value system that breeds irrefutable respect and unparalleled success. This is the living example. While this story is powerful and inspiring, its presentation is equally so. Chuck Warner is the preeminent author in the world of swimming and masterfully intertwines the extraordinary success of Coach Reese with the powerful virtues that laid the groundwork for that success."

—DON HEIDARY, Past Board President, The American Swimming Coaches Association, Co-Head Coach/Founder, Orinda Aquatics

Available in hard and soft cover on
CHUCKWARNERBOOKS.COM
and soft cover on Amazon.
Also available as an audiobook on
BlackstoneLibrary.com and Amazon.

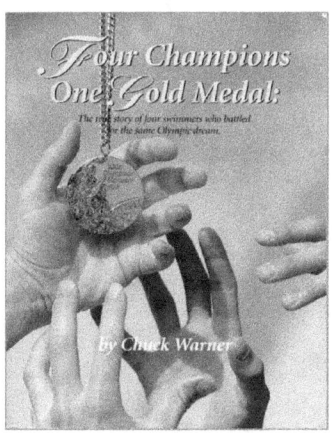

The story of Brian Goodell, Bobby Hackett, Stephen Holland, and Tim Shaw. The book chronicles their beginning in swimming all the way through the battle for the Olympic Gold Medal in the 1500-meter freestyle at the 1976 Olympic Games. Their performances from almost fifty years ago would still be competitive today. The boys were just sixteen to nineteen years of age.

"I have read many, many books on the sport of swimming, but this is the first I've read in the 'can't put it down' until finished category…a 'must-read' for anyone interested in the health and future of competitive swimming."

—DENNIS PURSLEY, US National Team Director

Available at Amazon and WWW.CHUCKWARNERBOOKS.COM

www.ingramcontent.com/pod-product-compliance
Lightning Source LLC
LaVergne TN
LVHW010558070526
838199LV00063BA/5004